OhSewEasy®

duvet covers & curtains

15 Projects for Stylish Living

Jean & Valori Wells

C&T PUBLISHING

Text © 2006 Jean Wells and Valori Wells

Artwork © 2006 C&T Publishing, Inc.

Publisher: Amy Marson

Editorial Director: Gailen Runge

Acquisitions Editor: Jan Grigsby

Editor: Candie Frankel

Technical Editors: Elin Thomas, Robyn Gronning

Copyeditor/Proofreader: Wordfirm, Inc.

Design Director/Cover/Book Designer: Kristy K. Zacharias

Illustrator: Kirstie L. Pettersen

Production Assistant: Kerry Graham

Photography: Diane Pedersen and Luke Mulks, unless otherwise noted

Published by C&T Publishing, Inc., PO Box 1456, Lafayette, CA 94549

Front cover: Four-by-Four Duvet Cover with coordinating pillows

Back cover: Tossed Rectangles Duvet Cover, Classic Duvet Cover and Ruffled Bedskirt, Patchwork Shower Curtain

Library of Congress Cataloging-in-Publication Data

Wells, Jean.

   Oh sew easy duvet covers & curtains : 15 projects for stylish living / Jean and Valori Wells.

      p. cm.

   Includes index.

   ISBN-13: 978-1-57120-358-8 (paper trade)

   ISBN-10: 1-57120-358-3 (paper trade)

   1. Household linens. 2. Coverlets. 3. Curtains. I. Wells, Valori. II. Title.

   TT387.W47 2006

   646.2'1--dc22

                                        2006001149

Printed in China

10 9 8 7 6 5 4 3 2 1

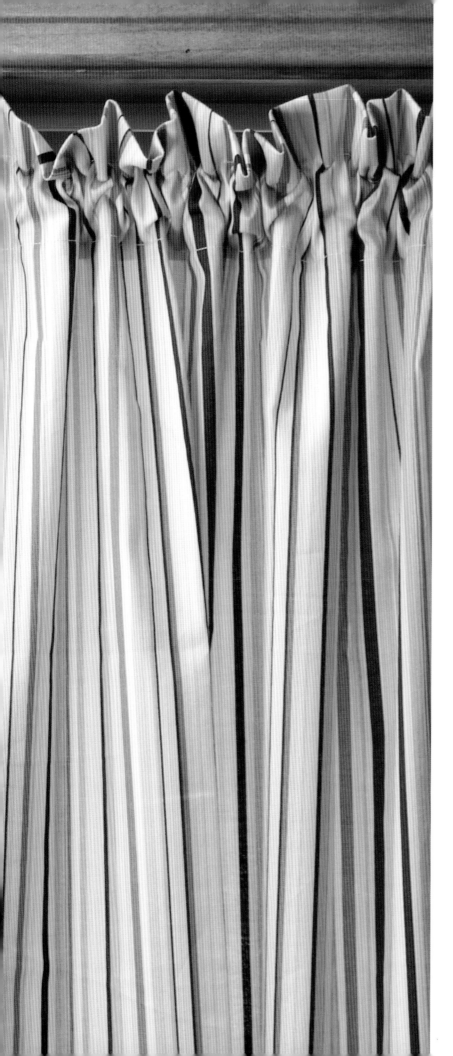

acknowledgments

Putting together a book is a team effort. Although we came up with the ideas, we welcomed help from some "sewing fairies" toward the end of the project. We want to thank Annette Caldwell, Carolyn Spencer, Lawry Thorn, and Jeanne Sellgren for sewing up a storm when needed.

Valori and Ross's new baby daughter, Olivia Rose, decided to arrive the day before our scheduled three-day photo shoot. Carolyn Spencer stepped in for Valori to help Jean style the photos and set up and take down each shot. We love working with C&T photographer Luke Mulks. He has a great eye and helps us achieve the look and style we want in our photographs.

The homes where we photographed the projects helped us create the style of this book. We want to thank Janet and Peter Storton, Carolyn and Eric Spencer, Andrea and Jeremy Storton, and our husbands for letting us disrupt their homes and daily routine in order to photograph. The flowers came from our gardens.

Working on another book with Candie Frankel is a true joy. We each understand how the other works, and our complementary skills make our many tasks that much easier to accomplish. Elin Thomas contributed her technical editing expertise, and Kristy Zacharias once again brought our words and photos together in a beautiful format designed to appeal to today's new generation of sewers.

And finally, our continuing appreciation to Todd Hensley and the C&T family for believing in our series of soft furnishings project books and making them happen.

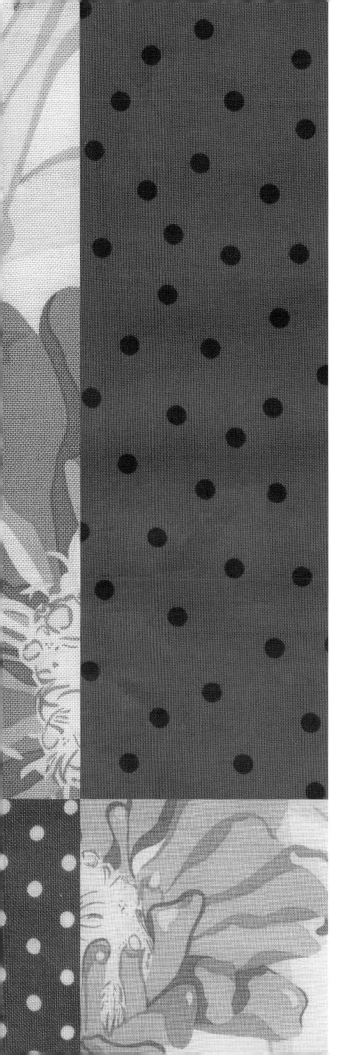

contents

introduction

Walk into any bedroom and the first thing that grabs your eye is the bed and its bedding. Windows and window treatments draw similar attention. Bed and window decor poses particular challenges to the home sewer because of the sheer volume of fabric that is required. After investing in a large amount of fabric, you might be nervous about making a cutting or sewing mistake that you cannot correct.

In this second book in our Oh Sew Easy series, we'll look at duvet covers and curtains that are big on style and decorating impact but geared to the skills of the beginner to intermediate sewer. You'll learn how to sew duvet covers for all the bed sizes in your home, from twin to king. For curtain-making, we give you a fill-in-the-blanks worksheet to help you calculate fabric yardage and curtain panel sizes with confidence. Our goal is not to bring you prepackaged, one-size-fits-all projects but to help you develop and apply your sewing skills so that you can decorate real rooms in your unique home!

We were fortunate to be able to photograph each duvet cover we designed in the room setting for which it was made. You will see a gardenlike setting, a Tuscan color scheme with a folk art touch, a playful child's room with a cat and dog theme, a classic craftsman look, a modern style, and a vintage bedroom. We developed these decorating themes with accessories from The Wild Hare, our home and gift store in Sisters, Oregon. Then we added pillows of all styles, shapes, and sizes, borrowing ideas and patterns from our sister title, *Oh Sew Easy Pillows*. (For a complete look at pillow-making, don't miss this marvelous book!)

Our curtains are easy-to-make styles similar to those you might find in today's decorating magazines and home furnishings catalogs. We have kept the instructions simple yet have included enough details for you to mix and match elements and develop your own designs. These simple, elegant styles, sewn in the fabrics of your choice and paired with today's eclectic hardware, will go a long way toward creating whatever ambiance spells "home" for you.

Valori, a novice sewer of items for the home, found these duvet cover and curtain projects extremely easy to make. Another surprise is that they are less time-consuming than the quilt projects she usually undertakes. For Jean, sewing for the home has been its own sort of homecoming. Projects like these bring her back to the type of sewing she did years ago when she was furnishing her first home.

Both of us have had a great time planning the styles, choosing the fabrics, and putting together exciting, distinct room settings for this idea-packed book. Let us know how you like it!

Jean & *Valori*

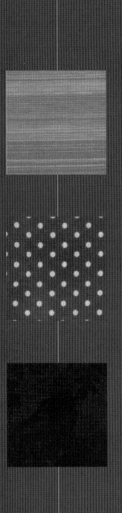

duvet covers

A duvet cover is like a giant pillowcase that is used to cover and protect a comforter.

Duvet covers can be removed for laundering. They are convenient in other ways, too. Instead of owning several bulky comforters in different styles or colors, you can invest in just one comforter and make a wardrobe of duvet covers for it.

The duvet cover offers the perfect opportunity to create or change the ambiance in a bedroom. The style of the duvet cover can be tailored, romantic, contemporary, formal, informal, or rustic, depending on the fabric, trims, and closure that you choose. Your lifestyle, personal taste, and perhaps the decor in other areas of your home will influence the direction (or directions!) you choose to go.

In this chapter, we show you how to select the right size comforter for your twin-, full-, queen-, or king-size bed and how to sew a simple, classic duvet cover for it. We also show you different closure options to use on the open end of the duvet cover. We finish with a bonus: two easy-to-sew bedskirt styles to conceal the box spring and complete your bed ensemble.

The Comforter

A comforter is made of two pieces of fabric that surround and protect an insert filled with polyester or down. The comforter covers the mattress and hangs down past the thickness of the mattress at the sides and foot of the bed.

If you are purchasing a new comforter, measure the length and width of the top of the mattress and the mattress thickness. Add two mattress thicknesses to the width and one mattress thickness to the length to arrive at your measurements. These are the dimensions of a comforter that will cover the top of the bed and drop down on three sides to conceal the edges of the mattress.

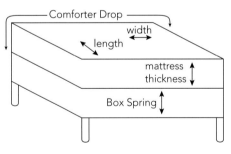

In an informal survey of bedding catalogs and retail bedding stores, we found an array of comforter sizes. For this book, we decided to design duvet covers to fit the comforter sizes outlined in C&T's publication *All-in-One Quilter's Reference Tool* (and listed in the Sizes chart, above right). If your comforter measures an inch or two wider or narrower than these dimensions, don't worry—it will still fit inside the duvet covers featured in this book. You have some leeway because a duvet cover isn't designed to fit like a glove. You can make adjustments on the outer edges if you like, but it is not absolutely necessary.

Sizes

BED SIZE	MATTRESS SIZE	COMFORTER SIZE
Twin	39″ × 75″	63″ × 87″
Double/Full	54″ × 75″	78″ × 87″
Queen	60″ × 80″	84″ × 92″
King	78″ × 80″	102″ × 92″

Some Useful Tools

- Calculator
- Yardstick or long ruler
- Seam gauge: Use this 6″ ruler with movable guide to mark the space you are measuring.
- Chalk pencils to mark dark fabrics
- Lead pencils to mark light fabrics

A Basic Duvet Cover
the front

Even if it is for a twin bed, a duvet cover takes a lot of yardage. Most fabrics are simply not wide enough to span the width of the comforter. The simple solution is to cut three panels of fabric and sew them together to obtain the required width. The panel in the middle is wider than the two panels at the sides. This design, used for many commercially manufactured duvet covers, avoids a seam down the middle and looks balanced on the bed.

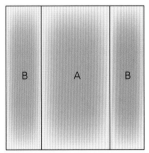
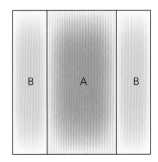

Duvet Cover Front   Duvet Cover Front Variation

A variation on this construction is to sew the duvet cover from two different fabrics, one for center panel A and another for the B side panels.

The width and length of panels A and B are based on the comforter size. (The measurements are for finished pieces. The pieces are cut 1″ larger.)

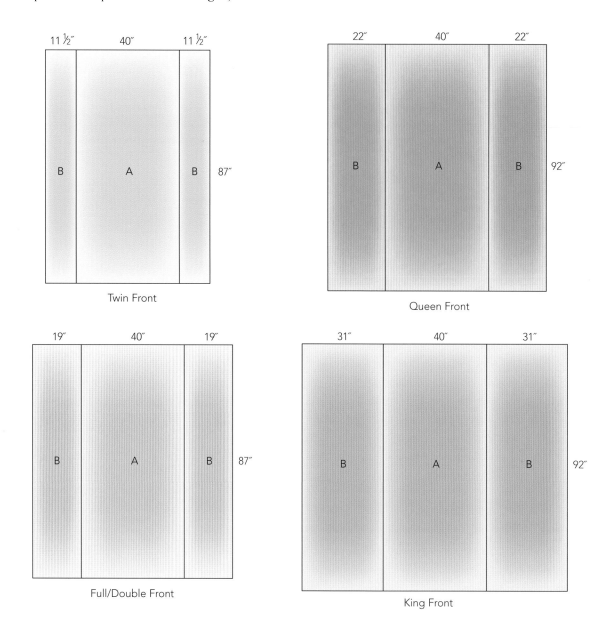

11 ½″	40″	11 ½″
B	A	B

87″

Twin Front

22″	40″	22″
B	A	B

92″

Queen Front

19″	40″	19″
B	A	B

87″

Full/Double Front

31″	40″	31″
B	A	B

92″

King Front

Tip

The yardage charts for the projects in this book assume a 42″ usable fabric width. If your fabric is wider, recalculate the width of the panels to see if you can sew a similar layout with less yardage. Another option is to sew your left-over fabrics into pillows, cushions, and other decorating accessories.

The projects in this book feature a variety of design layouts for the front of the duvet cover. We hope you enjoy trying them all.

the back

The back of the duvet cover can be made in the same fabric as the front or in a different fabric. The measurements below are for a basic duvet cover. You can use this as a guideline for piecing. The projects vary slightly in size, so follow the measurements and yardage requirements for the specific projects. Sometimes you can cut the two B panels for queen-size backs from one length of fabric; depending on the width of the back, you might need two lengths.

For a twin-size duvet cover, use two B panels seamed down the middle. Unless the comforter is reversible, this seam will not be noticeable when the duvet is on the bed.for queen-size backs from one length of fabric; depending on the width of the back, you might need two lengths.

Back Panels Cutting Guide

DUVET COVER SIZE	PANEL A	PANEL B (cut 2)	PANEL C (cut 2)
Twin	—	32½″ × 88″	—
Full/Double	41″ × 88″	20″ × 88″	—
Queen	41″ × 93″	23″ × 93″	—
King	41″ × 93″	32″ × 93″	—
King (Variation)	41″ × 93″	21″ × 93″	12″ × 93″

Making Space

Duvet covers use voluminous amounts of fabric. To make cutting and measuring easier and more accurate, work on a large table or clear an ample workspace on the floor.

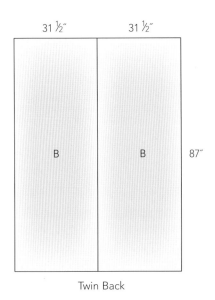

Twin Back

Full-size and queen-size backs are sewn from one A and two B panels.

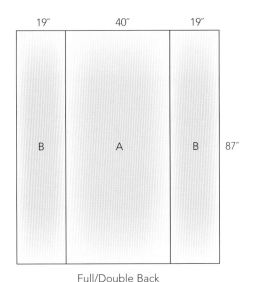

Full/Double Back

Queen Back

For a king-size back, you can use one A and two B panels (the yardage given in the projects) or one A, two B, and two C panels. The second option makes more economical use of the fabric. Begin by cutting two A panels. Cut one of the A panels in half lengthwise to make two B panels. To make the C panels with minimal fabric waste, cut five 12″ × 42″ strips on the crosswise grain. Piece them together into one long strip, using ½″ seams. Press the seam allowances. Subcut the strip into two 12″ × 93″ panels. By choosing an accent fabric for the C panels, you can add a design on the back for a reversible duvet cover.

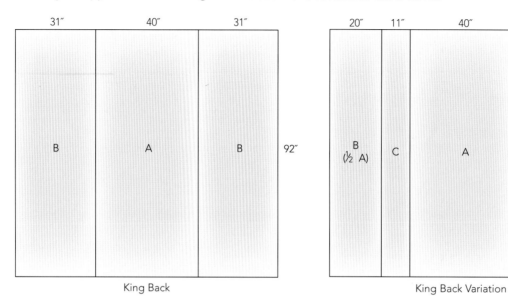

King Back

King Back Variation

sewing the duvet cover

Sew all seams using a ½″ seam allowance. Cut off about ½″ from each long edge of the fabric panels to remove the selvages before seaming them together. Construct the front of the duvet cover first and measure it, as you may need to modify the panel measurements of the back to match.

Front: Lay out the A and B panels as shown in the duvet cover front diagram (page 12). Place a B panel along each long edge of the A panel, right sides together. Align and pin the ends and the center of the long edges and add pins every few inches, keeping the panels even. Sew the panels together and press the seam allowances toward B.

Back: Lay out the A and B panels (or A, B, and C panels for the king-size variation) as shown in the appropriate duvet back diagram (page 13 or above). Pin and sew the panels to one another, right sides

together, along the long edges. Press the seam allowances.

Assembly: Place the front and back pieces right sides together and pin. Stitch the side and top edges only. Leave the bottom edge open.

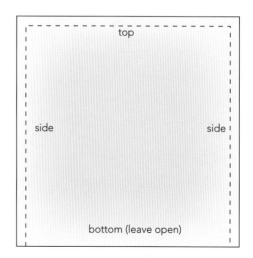

Joining the front and back

Closures

The opening at the bottom of the duvet cover can be closed in one of several ways. Buttons and buttonholes are the most popular and will give your duvet cover a European look. Ties are an easy and inexpensive alternative, since you can sew them from leftover fabric. Hidden closure options include sew-in snaps, Velcro hook-and-loop fastener dots, and sew-in snap tapes. Snap tape is sturdy, makes a durable closure, and is easy to install, but it can get pricey when you tally up the cost per yard. A final option is to install a zipper.

edge facing

With the exception of the zipper, every closure option in this book requires a facing on the bottom open edge of the duvet cover. The facing encloses and finishes the raw edge, giving the duvet cover a stylish trim. The resulting double layer of fabric makes whatever closure you choose sturdier.

1. Follow the project instructions to cut the facing strips.

2. Sew the facing strips end to end, right sides together, to make one long strip. Press the seam allowances. Trim the strip to measure:

Twin: 127″   Full/Double: 157″

Queen: 169″   King: 205″

3. Sew the ends together to make a loop and press.

4. Press one edge of the facing loop ½″ to the wrong side.

5. Place the facing on the duvet cover with right sides together and raw edges matching. Pin. Stitch ½″ from the edge all around.

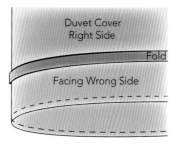

Joining the facing

6. Open out and press the seam allowance toward the facing.

7. Turn the facing to the inside of the duvet cover so that the pressed-in fold just covers the previous stitching line.

8. Press and topstitch along the folded edge through all layers.

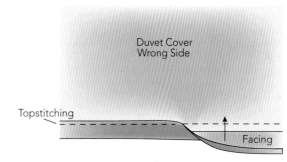

Topstitching

For a playful look, choose buttons that contrast with the fabric.

button and buttonhole closure

Use flat ⅝″ two-hole or four-hole buttons for this functional closure. Avoid shank buttons, as they sit too high off the surface. The buttonholes are spaced 5″ to 6″ apart in a facing.

1. Lay the duvet cover on a flat surface, as if you were placing it on a bed. Align the folded edges of the facing, so that the part of the facing that is attached to the duvet front is on top of the part of the facing that is attached to the duvet back.

2. Insert pins along the top facing to mark the buttonhole placement, following the project instructions. The buttonholes should be evenly spaced, about 5″ to 6″ apart.

3. Set your sewing machine to make a ⅝″ buttonhole, as described in your machine's instruction manual. Sew a buttonhole at each pin marker in the top facing only.

4. Place a button on the inside edge of the lower facing to correspond to each buttonhole.

5. Sew the buttons in place, carrying the stitches through to the outside of the facing for a secure hold.

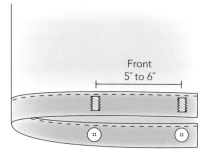

Front
5″ to 6″

Buttons and Buttonholes

Tip

If you love the look of buttons but hate making buttonholes, then this tip is for you. Sew the buttons to the outside of the top facing (not the bottom facing). Then sew some Velcro dots or small snaps on the inside edges of the facing, where they'll be concealed.

Tie closures are casual, playful, and easy for beginners to make.

tie closure

1. Complete steps 1–4 of Edge Facing (see page 15).

2. Cut 12 or more strips, each 2″ × 9″, from the fabric or fabrics of your choice.

3. Fold in one end of each strip ¼″ to the wrong side and press.

4. Fold each strip in half lengthwise, right side out. Press to set a crease. Open the strip and fold each raw edge toward the center fold. Refold all the layers and press well. Topstitch the long open edge.

Press in half and open out   Fold to middle

Topstitch

5. Lay the duvet cover right side out on a flat surface, as if you were placing it on a bed. Align the raw open edges, so that the duvet front is on top of the duvet back.

6. Place 6 ties on the duvet front, raw edges matching and spaced evenly apart. Pin in place through the duvet front only. Pin the remaining 6 ties to the outside of the duvet back to correspond to the ties on the duvet front.

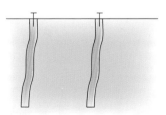

7. Complete step 5 of Edge Facing, enclosing the ties in the seam.

8. Complete steps 6–7 of Edge Facing.

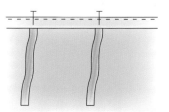

This zipper closure is concealed by piping sewn into the seam.

zipper closure

Long zippers are sometimes hard to find and are limited to a few basic colors. Still, we like zipper closures because they make the duvet tight and snug, like a pillow. The zipper doesn't have to span the entire lower edge. A zipper 38″ to 48″ long provides a large enough opening for inserting and removing the comforter. Sew and assemble the duvet front and back as directed in the project instructions, but leave the last 1″ at the bottom unsewn.

1. Trim ½″ from the back bottom edge of the duvet cover.

2. Turn the new edge under ½″ and press.

3. Cut strips of fabric 1½″ wide, enough to fit across the back bottom edge. Stitch together into one long piece. Press in ½″ along the length, wrong sides together.

4. Center the zipper on the pressed edge of the duvet cover and place pins at the beginning and end to mark the zipper length.

5. Place the opened-out ½″ raw edge of the long folded strip of fabric and the back bottom edge of the duvet right sides together. Stitch together on the fold from each end until you reach the pin. Backtack. Repeat at the other end of the duvet cover, leaving open the part where the zipper will be placed.

6. Press the seam open. Center the zipper under the opening and pin in place. With a zipper foot on the sewing machine, topstitch the zipper to the fabric, as shown.

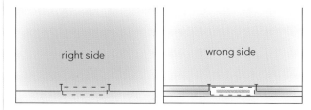

right side   wrong side

7. Open the zipper. Put the raw edges of the duvet front and back right sides together and stitch a ½″ seam. Turn the cover right side out through the zipper.

Bedskirts

A bedskirt hides the box spring under the mattress and dresses up the bed. You could simply put a fitted sheet on the box spring, but a bedskirt adds panache. Choose a fabric that complements the duvet and enhances the room decor.

Bedskirts can be gathered or tailored. Begin by measuring the width and length of the box spring with a tape measure. Add two lengths and one width to determine the running length of the bedskirt. These measurements correspond to the sides and foot of the box spring, where the bedskirt will be attached. (Note that there is no bedskirt at the head of the bed.) For the drop, measure from the top of the box spring to the floor. Jot down your measurements.

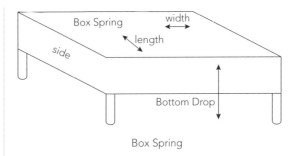

Box Spring

The bedskirt is attached to a panel that covers the top of the box spring. To make this panel, we like to use a flat sheet trimmed to the same size as the box spring. This part of the bedskirt construction remains hidden from view, so it can be any color. Place a hemmed edge of the flat sheet along the edge of the box spring that will touch the headboard or wall.

In the steps that follow, use a calculator as needed and jot down your results as you go.

ruffled bedskirt

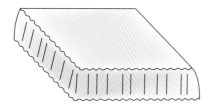

1. Multiply the bedskirt running length (2 lengths and 1 width of the box spring) by 2 to allow for the gathers.

2. Divide your step 1 result by the fabric width. Round up or down to the nearest whole number to determine the number of bedskirt panels you will need to cut.

3. Add $1\frac{1}{2}''$ to the box spring drop measurement. This measurement is the depth of each bedskirt panel.

4. Multiply your step 2 result by your step 3 result. Divide by $36''$ to determine the fabric yardage. Round up to the nearest $\frac{1}{8}$ yard. Allow extra yardage if the fabric has a printed pattern repeat that you want to match.

5. Cut the required number of panels (step 2) from the fabric yardage. Each panel measures the fabric width × the panel depth (step 3). Cut the selvages off each end before seaming them.

6. Sew the panels together end to end along the short edges, using a $\frac{1}{2}''$ seam allowance. Press the seams open. Turn the short edges $\frac{1}{4}''$ to the back and press. Turn again $\frac{1}{2}''$ and topstitch to hem the ends.

7. Turn up the bottom edge $\frac{1}{2}''$ and press. Turn up another $\frac{1}{2}''$ and press to make a double-fold hem. Topstitch on the fold.

8. Machine baste $\frac{1}{4}''$ and $\frac{1}{2}''$ from the long raw edge. Hold the bobbin basting threads together at one end and pull gently, gathering the edge to fit the side and bottom edges of the flat sheet panel. Adjust the gathers so they are evenly distributed.

9. Pin the bedskirt to the side and bottom edges of the panel, right sides together. Stitch between the gathering stitches to join the skirt to the panel.

tailored bedskirt

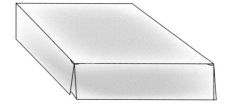

1. Add $16''$ to the bedskirt running length (2 lengths and 1 width of the box spring).

2. Follow steps 2–5 of Ruffled Bedskirt (left) to calculate the yardage. Cut the panels.

3. Follow step 6 of Ruffled Bedskirt to join the panels and hem the ends.

4. Follow step 7 of Ruffled Bedskirt to hem the lower edge.

5. Pin the bedskirt to the side and bottom edges of the top panel, right sides together. At each corner, fold a $4''$ inverted box pleat and pin. Match the ends and middle of the side and bottom sections and pin securely. Stitch around 3 sides, securing the pleats at each corner as you go.

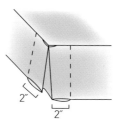

Inverted Box Pleat

Examples

A queen-size box spring measures $60'' \times 80''$ and has an $18''$ drop.

For a **ruffled bedskirt**, the total length is $440''$ and the depth is $19\frac{1}{2}''$. This style requires ten panels, each $19\frac{1}{2}'' \times 42''$, cut from $5\frac{1}{2}$ yards of fabric.

For a **tailored bedskirt**, the total length is $236''$ and the depth is $19\frac{1}{2}''$. This style requires six panels, each $19\frac{1}{2}'' \times 42''$, cut from $3\frac{1}{2}$ yards of fabric.

duvet cover •

recipes

classic duvet cover

This simple, elegant duvet cover was made for Janet Storton from a 1927 vintage fabric that she purchased at an antique store. Carefully matched printed patterns make the seams between the A and B panels virtually invisible. Janet chose to pipe the edge in a contrasting color for yet another classy touch. (Consult *Oh Sew Easy Pillows*, our companion book in the Oh Sew Easy series, for complete piping instructions.)

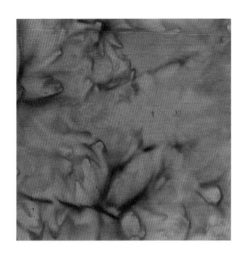

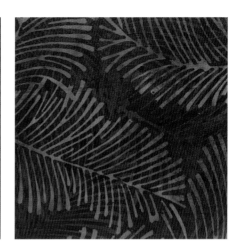

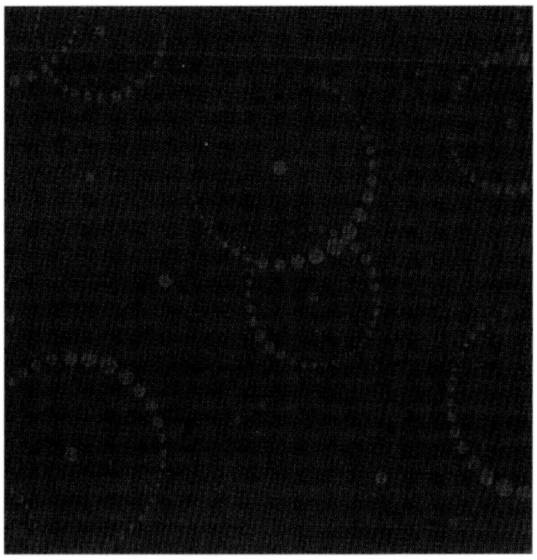

Materials

Choose the style options you desire from the table below. Make the duvet front using a single fabric for panels A and B or one fabric for A and another fabric for B. Close the duvet cover with buttons or a zipper.

DUVET SIZE	FABRIC FOR A, B, AND FACING	FABRIC FOR A ONLY	FABRIC FOR B AND FACING ONLY	BACK FABRIC	$\frac{5}{8}''$ BUTTONS	OR	36" OR 48" ZIPPER
Twin	5¼ yards	2¾ yards	2⅞ yards	5 yards	12		1
Full	5¼ yards	2¾ yards	2⅞ yards	5 yards	15		1
Queen	8¼ yards	2¾ yards	5¾ yards	8 yards	16		1
King	8¼ yards	2¾ yards	5¾ yards	8 yards	18		1

Cutting Guide

DUVET SIZE	PANEL A (cut 1)	PANEL B (cut 2)	FACING STRIPS 2½" × 42"	BACK PANELS
Twin	41" × 88"	12½" × 88"	Cut 4	32½" × 88" (cut 2)
Full	41" × 88"	20" × 88"	Cut 4	41" × 88" (cut 1) 20" × 88" (cut 2)
Queen	41" × 93"	23" × 93"	Cut 5	41" × 93" (cut 1) 23" × 93" (cut 2)
King	41" × 93"	32" × 93"	Cut 5	41" × 93" (cut 1) 32" × 93" (cut 2)

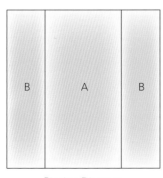

Piecing Diagram

Sew all seams using a ½" seam allowance.

FRONT: Lay out the A and B panels as shown in the piecing diagram. Sew a B panel to each long edge of the A panel, right sides together. Press the seam allowances toward B.

BACK: Follow the Back sewing instructions on page 14.

ASSEMBLY: Follow the Assembly sewing instructions on page 14.

CLOSURE: Follow the Closures sewing instructions on pages 15–16 or page 18.

panel duvet cover

The vertical panels in this duvet cover are easy to sew. The twin cover has three panels and the full, queen, and king sizes have five panels each. Several decorative variations can be explored in this style, depending on how many fabrics you want to combine. For an easygoing design, try two fabrics that alternate. For an eclectic look, make every panel different. If you favor symmetry in the five-panel version, try a feature fabric in the middle and two more fabrics flanking the sides. In our example, we chose two fabrics for the panels and inserted a third fabric in an accent color in narrow bands along the seams.

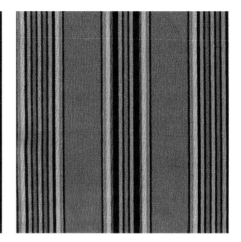

Materials

The panels can be cut on the lengthwise or crosswise grain of the fabric. Cutting on the crosswise grain makes more economical use of the fabric, but you will need to sew together smaller sections to achieve the required panel length. If the extra seams will bother you, buy more fabric and cut the pieces on the lengthwise grain. You can use the leftover pieces to make accent pillows and other accessories.

DUVET SIZE	FABRIC FOR A:		FABRIC FOR B:		ACCENT FABRIC	BACK FABRIC AND FACING	$\frac{5}{8}$″ BUTTONS
	LENGTHWISE CUT	CROSSWISE CUT	LENGTHWISE CUT	CROSSWISE CUT			
Twin	$2\frac{5}{8}$ yards	2 yards	5 yards	$3\frac{1}{4}$ yards	$\frac{1}{3}$ yard	$5\frac{1}{3}$ yards	12
Full	5 yards	$3\frac{1}{2}$ yards	$2\frac{5}{8}$ yards	$2\frac{1}{2}$ yards	$\frac{5}{8}$ yard	$5\frac{1}{3}$ yards	15
Queen	$5\frac{1}{3}$ yards	$3\frac{5}{8}$ yards	$2\frac{2}{3}$ yards	$2\frac{5}{8}$ yards	$\frac{5}{8}$ yard	$8\frac{1}{4}$ yards	16
King	$7\frac{7}{8}$ yards	$4\frac{1}{2}$ yards	$5\frac{1}{3}$ yards	$3\frac{1}{4}$ yards	$\frac{5}{8}$ yard	$8\frac{1}{3}$ yards	18

Cutting Guide

DUVET SIZE	FABRIC FOR A:		FABRIC FOR B:		ACCENT STRIPS	FACING STRIPS	BACK PANELS
	LENGTHWISE CUT	CROSSWISE CUT	LENGTHWISE CUT	CROSSWISE CUT	CROSSWISE CUT	$2\frac{1}{2}$″ × 42″	
Twin	22″ × 88″ (cut 1)	22″ × 42″ (cut 3)	22″ × 88″ (cut 2)	22″ × 42″ (cut 5)	$1\frac{3}{4}$″ × 42″ (cut 5)	Cut 4	$32\frac{1}{2}$″ × 88″ (cut 2)
Full	17″ × 88″ (cut 3)	17″ × 42″ (cut 7)	17″ × 88″ (cut 2)	17″ × 42″ (cut 5)	$1\frac{3}{4}$″ × 42″ (cut 9)	Cut 4	41″ × 88″ (cut 1) 21″ × 88″ (cut 2)
Queen	18″ × 93″ (cut 3)	18″ × 42″ (cut 7)	18″ × 93″ (cut 2)	18″ × 42 (cut 5)	$1\frac{3}{4}$″ × 42″ (cut 10)	Cut 5	41″ × 93″ (cut 1) $23\frac{1}{2}$″ × 93″ (cut 2)
King	22″ × 93″ (cut 3)	22″ × 42″ (cut 7)	22″ × 93″ (cut 2)	22″ × 42″ (cut 5)	$1\frac{3}{4}$″ × 42″ (cut 10)	Cut 6	41″ × 93″ (cut 1) $33\frac{1}{2}$″ × 93″ (cut 2)

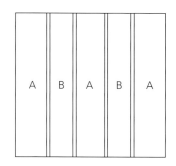

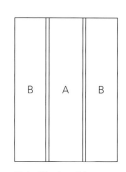

| A | B | A | B | A |

| B | A | B |

Full, Queen, and King Piecing Diagram

Twin Piecing Diagram

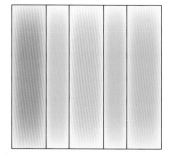

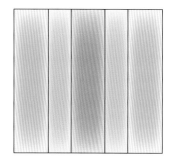

Design Variations

Sew all seams using a ½″ seam allowance.

PANELS (CROSSWISE CUT ONLY): Sew the crosswise-cut A panel pieces end to end. Press the seam allowances open. Subcut into A panels that match the lengthwise cut dimensions listed in the Cutting Guide. Repeat to make the B panels.

ACCENT STRIPS: Sew the accent strips end to end. Press the seam allowances open. Subcut into 2 strips (twin size) or 4 strips (full, queen, and king sizes); make the strips the same length as panels A and B. Fold each strip in half lengthwise, right side out, and press.

FRONT: Lay out the A and B panels as shown in the piecing diagram. Pin an accent strip to every inside long edge of the A panels. Layer the A and B panels, right sides together, and stitch, catching the accent strips in the seams. Press the seam allowances toward B and the accent strips toward A.

BACK: Follow the Back sewing instructions on page 14.

ASSEMBLY: Follow the Assembly sewing instructions on page 14.

CLOSURE: Follow the Closures sewing instructions for facing, buttons, and buttonholes on pages 15–16.

nine-patch duvet cover

Nine rectangles joined with narrow sashing strips make up the design of this floral duvet cover. The large print is a perfect scale for a bed. To play up the bold geometric pattern, try three different fabrics placed in different color block combinations. Fabric ties are used for the bottom closing.

  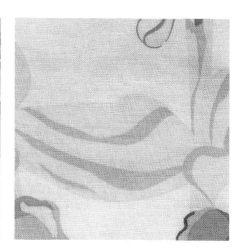

Materials

Choose the style options you desire from the table below. The blocks can be cut from a single fabric or from three different fabrics. Add the yardage amounts for sashing, facing, and ties if you wish to cut these from a single fabric.

DUVET SIZE	BLOCK FABRIC		SASHING	FACING	BACK	TIES
	ONE FABRIC	THREE DIFFERENT FABRICS				
Twin	5⅝ yards	2 yards each	⅝ yard	⅜ yard	5 yards	¼ yard
Full	6⅞ yards	2⅜ yards each	⅝ yard	⅜ yard	5 yards	¼ yard
Queen	7⅛ yards	2½ yards each	⅝ yard	½ yard	5⅓ yards	¼ yard
King	7⅞ yards	2⅔ yards each	¾ yard	⅝ yard	7¾ yards	¼ yard

Cutting Guide

DUVET SIZE	BLOCK FABRIC		SASHING STRIPS 2″ × 42″	FACING STRIPS 2½″ × 42″	BACK PANELS	TIE STRIPS 2″ × 42″
	ONE FABRIC (cut 9)	THREE FABRICS (cut 3 of each)				
Twin	22″ × 29″ *	22″ × 29″	Cut 8	Cut 4	33″ × 87″ (cut 2)	Cut 3
Full	27″ × 29″ *	27″ × 29″	Cut 9	Cut 4	41″ × 87″ (cut 1) 20″ × 87″ (cut 2)	Cut 3
Queen	28″ × 31″ *	28″ × 31″	Cut 9	Cut 5	41″ × 93″ (cut 1) 22½″ × 93″ (cut 2)	Cut 3
King	35″ × 31″	35″ × 31″	Cut 10	Cut 6	41″ × 93″ (cut 1) 33″ × 93″ (cut 2)	Cut 3

* These blocks are cut crosswise to make the best use of yardage.

Piecing Diagram

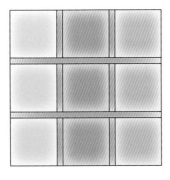

Design Variations

Sew all seams using a $\frac{1}{2}$″ seam allowance.

SASHING STRIPS: Sew the sashing strips end to end. Press the seam allowances open. Subcut into 6 strips 29″ for Twin/Full and 31″ for Queen/King. Cut the remaining sashing strip in half.

FRONT: Lay out the blocks in a nine-patch, referring to the piecing diagram or design variations. Place the sashing strips as shown in the piecing diagram. Stitch the blocks and vertical sashing strips together in rows. Press toward the sashing. Trim each horizontal sashing strip to match the row length. Join the rows and horizontal sashing. Press.

BACK: Follow the Back sewing instructions on page 14.

ASSEMBLY: Follow the Assembly sewing instructions on page 14.

CLOSURE: Follow the Closures sewing instructions for facing and ties on pages 15 and 17.

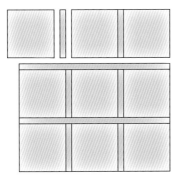

Row Piecing

medallion
duvet cover

The medallion duvet cover features a large rectangle of fabric in the center, surrounded by two bands of fabric. Our interpretation uses sophisticated prints in a wine and black palette. Other fabric combinations, such as brights or neutrals, would create quite different moods. Because the four comforter sizes—twin, full, queen, and king—are not proportional to one another, the center medallion is not the same shape in each. The diagrams will help you visualize how this design will look in the different sizes. The piecing sequence is the same for all four sizes.

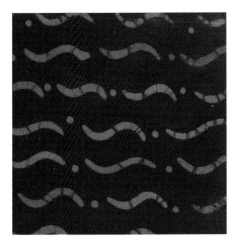

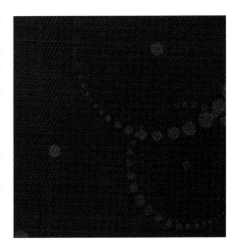

Materials

DUVET SIZE	FABRIC FOR A	FABRIC FOR B AND C	FABRIC FOR D, E, AND FACINGS	BACK	BUTTONS
Twin	1⅝ yards	⅔ yard	3½ yards	5 yards	12
Full	1⅜ yards	1 yard	4⅛ yards	5 yards	15
Queen	1⅛ yards	1⅛ yard	5⅛ yards	5⅓ yards	16
King	1½ yards	1⅜ yards	6⅝ yards	8½ yards	18

Cutting Guide

DUVET SIZE	A CENTER MEDALLION	B (cut crosswise)	C (cut crosswise)	D (cut crosswise)	E (cut crosswise)	FACING STRIPS 2½″ ×42″	BACK PANELS
Twin	28″ × 52″	4″ (cut 3)	4″ (cut 2)	16″ (cut 3)	16″ (cut 4)	Cut 4	Refer to the Back Panels Cutting Guide (page 13).
Full	35″ × 44″	5″ (cut 3)	5″ (cut 3)	19″ (cut 3)	19″ (cut 4)	Cut 4	
Queen	33″ × 41″ *	7″ (cut 2)	7″ (cut 3)	21″ (cut 3)	21″ (cut 5)	Cut 5	
King	47″ × 37″ *	9″ (cut 2)	9″ (cut 3)	24″ (cut 3)	24″ (cut 6)	Cut 6	

* These pieces are cut crosswise.

Border Piecing Guide

DUVET SIZE	INNER BORDERS B (make 2)	INNER BORDERS C (make 2)	OUTER BORDERS D (make 2)	OUTER BORDERS E (make 2)	BACK PANELS
Twin	4″ × 52″	4″ × 34″	16″ × 58″	16″ × 64″	32½″ × 88″ (cut 2)
Full	5″ × 44″	5″ × 43″	19″ × 52″	19″ × 79″	41″ × 88″ (cut 1) 20″ × 88″ (cut 2)
Queen	7″ × 41″	7″ × 45″	21″ × 53″	21″ × 85″	41″ × 93″ (cut 1) 23″ × 93″ (cut 2)
King	9″ × 37″	9″ × 63″	24″ × 53″	24″ × 109″	41″ × 99″ (cut 1) 35″ × 99″ (cut 2)

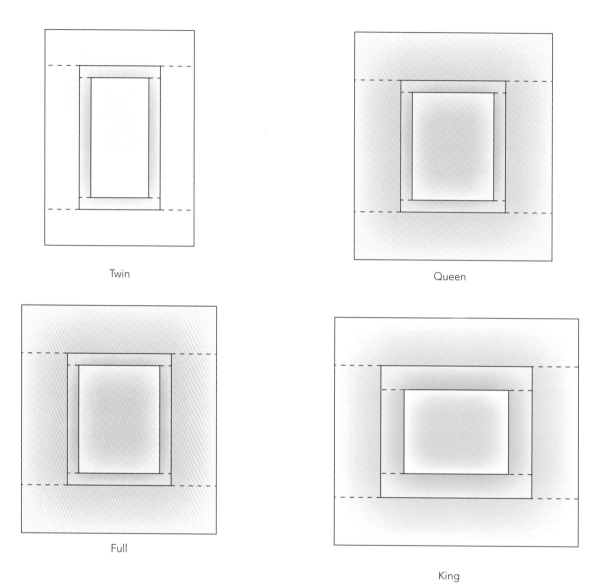

Twin

Queen

Full

King

Layout Diagrams

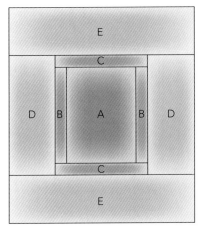

Piecing Diagram

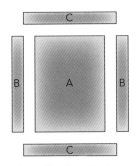

Inner Borders Piecing

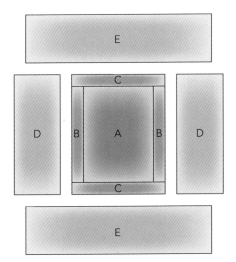

Outer Borders Piecing

Sew all seams using a $\frac{1}{2}$″ seam allowance.

BORDERS: Sew the B strips end to end. Press the seam allowances open. Refer to the border piecing guide to subcut 2 B inner borders to the dimensions listed. Make 2 C inner borders, 2 D outer borders, and 2 E outer borders in the same way.

FRONT: Lay out center medallion A and inner borders B and C as shown. Sew a B inner border to each side edge of A. Press toward B. Sew the C inner borders to the top and bottom edges. Press. Add the D outer borders. Press. Add the E outer borders. Press.

BACK: Follow the Back sewing instructions on page 14.

ASSEMBLY: Follow the Assembly sewing instructions on page 14.

CLOSURE: Follow the Closures sewing instructions for facing, buttons, and buttonholes on pages 15–16.

four-by-four
duvet cover

Sixteen rectangles are stitched together in rows of four to create this duvet cover. For her cover, Andrea Storton chose large floral and geometric prints with a contemporary flair. Be sure to spread out the lights and darks when arranging the rectangles to achieve a pleasing balance.

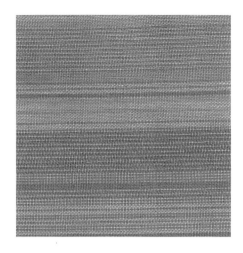

Materials

Make the majority of your blocks from your favorite fabric. Then cut the facing strips and ties from other block fabrics to coordinate.

DUVET SIZE	FABRIC FOR BLOCK 1	FABRIC FOR BLOCK 2	FABRIC FOR BLOCK 3	FABRIC FOR BLOCK 4	FABRIC FOR BLOCK 5	FABRIC FOR BLOCK 6	BACK
Twin	1⅜ yards	1⅜ yards	¾ yards	1⅜ yards	¾ yard	¾ yard	5 yards
Full	1⅜ yards	1⅜ yards	¾ yards	1⅜ yards	¾ yard	¾ yard	5 yards
Queen	2 yards	2⅝ yards	1⅓ yards	2 yards	1⅓ yard	1⅓ yard	8 yards
King	2⅛ yards	2¾ yards	1½ yards	2⅛ yards	1½ yard	1½ yard	8 yards

Cutting Guide

DUVET SIZE	BLOCK 1 (cut 3)	BLOCK 2 (cut 4)	BLOCK 3 (cut 2)	BLOCK 4 (cut 3)	BLOCK 5 (cut 2)	BLOCK 6 (cut 2)	FACING STRIPS 2½″ × 42″	BACK PANEL	TIES
Twin	16½″ × 22½″	16½″ × 22½″	16½″ × 22½″	16½″ × 22½″	16½″ × 22½″	16½″ × 22½″	Cut 4	32″ × 87″ (cut 2)	Cut 3 strips 2″ × 42″ from the leftover fabrics.
Full	20½″ × 22½″	20½″ × 22½″	20½″ × 22½″	20½″ × 22½″	20½″ × 22½″	20½″ × 22½″	Cut 4	41″ × 87″ (cut 1) 20″ × 87″ (cut 2)	
Queen	22″ × 24″ *	22″ × 24″ *	22″ × 24″ *	22″ × 24″ *	22″ × 24″ *	22″ × 24″ *	Cut 5	41″ × 92″ (cut 1) 23″ × 92″ (cut 2)	
King	26½″ × 24″	26½″ × 24″	26½″ × 24″	26½″ × 24″	26½″ × 24″	26½″ × 24″	Cut 5	41″ × 92″ (cut 1) 32″ × 92″ (cut 2)	

* These blocks are cut crosswise to make the best use of yardage.

1	2	3	4
5	6	1	2
2	3	4	6
4	1	2	5

Front Piecing Diagram

Sew all seams using a $\frac{1}{2}''$ seam allowance.

FRONT: Lay out 16 blocks in 4 rows of 4 blocks each. Refer to the piecing diagram for the block placement or design your own arrangement. Sew the blocks together in rows. Press the seams open. Join the rows. Press all the seams in one direction.

BACK: Follow the Back sewing instructions on page 14.

ASSEMBLY: Follow the Assembly sewing instructions on page 14.

CLOSURE: Follow the Closures sewing instructions for facing and ties on pages 15 and 17.

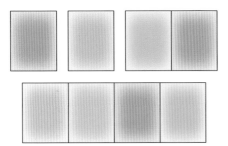

Sew the blocks in rows

tossed rectangles
duvet cover

Each rectangular block in this duvet cover is pieced from four smaller rectangles. When all nine blocks are joined, a lively pattern emerges. Panel A is rotated from side to side in the blocks to give the composition even more variety. A cat print and bright crayon colors make this duvet cover especially appealing for a child's bedroom.

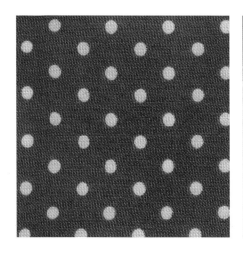

Materials

DUVET SIZE	ASSORTED FABRIC FOR A	ASSORTED FABRIC FOR B	ASSORTED FABRIC FOR C AND FACING	BACK	BUTTONS
Twin	1¾ yards total	2⅛ yards	2¾ yards	5 yards	12
Full	2⅝ yards total	2⅓ yards	2½ yards	7½ yards*	15
Queen	2¾ yards total	2¼ yards	3 yards	8 yards	16
King	2¾ yards total	2⅝ yards	3⅔ yards	8 yards	18

* If your useable fabric is 43″ or wider, you need 5 yards.

Cutting Guide

DUVET SIZE	A (cut 9 assorted)	B (cut 18 assorted)	C (cut 9 assorted)	FACING STRIPS 2½″ × 42″	BACK PANELS
Twin	8″ × 30″	8″ × 14″	15″ × 17″	Cut 4	32½″ × 88″ (cut 2)
Full	10″ × 30″	10″ × 16″	19″ × 15″	Cut 4	41″ × 88″ (cut 1) 21½″ × 88″ (cut 2)
Queen	11″ × 32″	11″ × 15″	21″ × 18″	Cut 5	41″ × 94″ (cut 1) 26″ × 94″ (cut 2)
King	13″ × 32″	13″ × 15″	25″ × 18″ *	Cut 5	41″ × 94″ (cut 1) 35″ × 94″ (cut 2)

* These blocks are cut crosswise to make the best use of yardage.

Block 1   Block 2

Sew all seams using a $1/2''$ seam allowance.

BLOCK 1: Lay out A, 2Bs, and C as shown in the block diagram. Sew the B pieces together along one long edge. Press the seam open. Sew C to the bottom edge of BB. Press toward C. Sew A to the left edge of BBC. Press toward A. Make 6 blocks.

Block 1 Piecing

BLOCK 2: Make a BBC unit, as you did for Block 1. Sew A to the right edge of BBC. Make 3 blocks.

Block 2 Piecing

FRONT: Lay out the blocks in 3 rows of 3 blocks each, as shown in the piecing diagram. Sew the blocks together in rows. Press the seams open. Join the rows. Press.

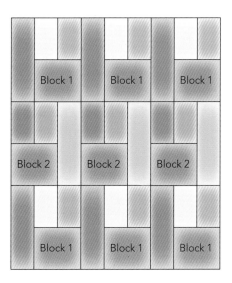

Piecing Diagram

BACK: Follow the Back sewing instructions on page 14.

ASSEMBLY: Follow the Assembly sewing instructions on page 14.

CLOSURE: Follow the Closures sewing instructions for facing, buttons, and buttonholes on pages 15–16.

Autumn Harvest Palette

See the Tossed Rectangles duvet cover in a sophisticated fabric palette on pages 8–9.

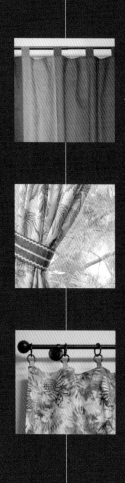

tab and rod pocket curtains

Curtains are casual, easygoing, and easy to make. They are essential elements in just about every decor, and sewers of all abilities can enjoy creating custom curtain designs for their homes.

curtain styles

Curtain With Rod Pocket, Outside Mount, Tiebacks

Curtain With Tabs, Outside Mount

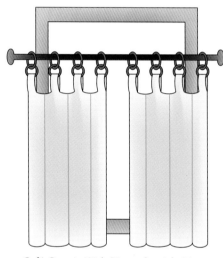

Café Curtain With Rings, Outside Mount

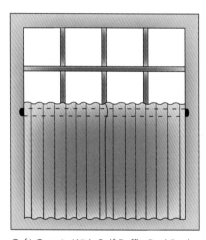

Café Curtain With Self Ruffle Rod Pocket,
Inside Mount

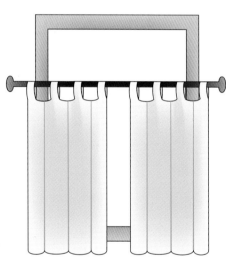

Café Curtain With Tabs, Outside Mount

header styles

Curtain With Rings

Rod Pocket

Rod Pocket With
Self Ruffle

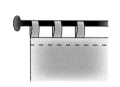

Tab Loops

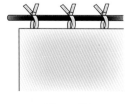

Tie-on Tabs

Making a curtain involves deciding on a curtain and header style, measuring the window, mounting the hardware, and sizing, cutting, and sewing the curtain panels. We'll look at each of these steps individually. The Curtain Recipes section features several curtain designs for you to try. We'll show you how to plug in your own measurements so you can adapt these designs for your own home.

The main features to consider in your curtain design are the header, the style and location of the mounting hardware, and the length of the panels. All of these features are interrelated. A decision you make about one feature will impact your choices for the other features.

The header is the part of the curtain panel that attaches to the curtain rod. Fabric tabs that slip onto the curtain rod are one option for the header. The tabs can be closed loops or the tie-on type. Another option is to sew purchased rings to the header. To open and close the curtains, you simply slide the tabs or rings along the rod. When the curtains are open, the panels fall in loose, informal folds.

The rod pocket, another header treatment, looks quite different from tabs. The pocket is a long, narrow channel formed by one or two rows of stitching along the length of the header. The curtain rod slides into this channel and is hidden from view, except where it emerges at the ends. The curtain panels are cut with extra fullness so that they shirr, or gather, when placed on the rod.

If the pocket is sewn using two stitching lines, the bit of header fabric that falls above the top stitching line forms a self ruffle when the curtain is gathered on the rod.

An attractive rod is a must for tab curtains, since so much of the rod remains visible. Most home supply stores and home furnishing catalogs have a variety of decorative rods and finials to choose from. For curtains with a rod pocket, you have the option of using a decorative rod or one that is strictly utilitarian.

Rods can be mounted outside or inside the window frame. Spring-loaded rods make inside mounts fast and easy to install. Rods that rest flush against the surface are appropriate for stationary window treatments, such as sheer curtains for a French door. A rod can be mounted at the top of the window opening or somewhere near or below the middle. Curtains that cover only the lower part of the window are called café curtains. This informal style provides privacy, yet admits plenty of light.

Measuring

You will need paper, pencil, chalk, and a retractable steel tape measure. Begin by drawing a sketch of your window on paper, referring to the diagram. As you work through the steps below, record your measurements on your sketch.

1. Decide the height at which you will mount the curtain rod and mark the spot on the wall with chalk.

2. Make a second mark where you would like the bottom hem of the curtain to fall.

3. Measure the vertical distance between the two marks and record it on your sketch as "length."

4. Decide on the rod length and mark each end on the wall with chalk. For an inside mount, the width is the same as the window opening. For an outside mount, the rod can extend beyond the window opening on each side. Extending the rod beyond the window frame will make the window appear wider than it actually is. When the curtains are opened all the way, they will cover the wall, not the window, and more light will enter the room. Record the rod measurement on your sketch as "width."

5. Follow the manufacturer's instructions to mount the curtain rod you have chosen. Repeat steps 1–4 to double-check your measurements.

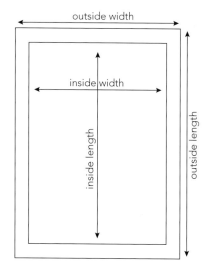

Tip

Not sure what length to hem your curtains? Here are some rules of thumb.

Inside mount: Let the bottom hem just touch the top of the windowsill.

Outside mount: Let the bottom hem reach 3″ to 4″ below the windowsill. For a long curtain, let the hem barely touch the floor.

Sizing the Panels

The length and width measurements you recorded are important, but you'll need to factor in other information before you can cut your fabric panels. Decide whether your curtains will be lined or unlined, and whether you want tabs, rings, or a rod pocket at the header. Before hemming, complete Worksheet lines 1–9 (page 46) to determine the panel size. We've filled in a sample worksheet (page 45) so that you can see how it's done. Our sample curtains are unlined tab curtains to be sewn from 42″-wide solid fabric.

After you calculate the panel size and yardage, cut the curtain fabric and lining (if using) into pieces that are the same length as your measurement from Worksheet line 9. Save the leftover curtain fabric for tabs and facings, as required. Cut approximately ½″ from each vertical edge of fabric to remove the selvages, which should not be sewn into the seams.

Sample Worksheet

PANEL SIZE	MY MEASUREMENTS AND CALCULATIONS (USE A CALCULATOR)
1. Enter your length measurement.	60″
2. Enter your width measurement.	30″
3. Measure the circumference of your curtain rod and add 1″.	4″
4. Circle the desired fullness. For tab curtains, allow 1½ or 2 times the width. This allows for some draping at the window when the curtains are drawn. For rod pocket curtains, allow 2 or 2½ times the width, or even more if the fabric is sheer.	1½ (2) 2½
5. Multiply line 2 by line 4.	60″
6. Do you want one or two panels? (circle one) One Panel Two Panels	1 OR (2)
7. Divide line 5 by line 6. The result is the finished panel width.	30″
8. Add two side hem allowances to line 7 (refer to the Hem Allowance chart on page 47). This is the panel width before hemming.	32½″
9. Add the top and bottom hem allowances to line 1 (refer to the Hem Allowance chart) and the rod measurement for rod pocket panels (your answer to line 3 above). This is the panel length before hemming.	64½″
FABRIC YARDAGE	
10. The width of your fabric is	42″
11. Using a calculator, divide line 8 by line 10. If the answer is 1 or less than 1, enter 1. If the answer is more than 1, round up to the nearest 0.5 decimal (1.5, 2.0, 2.5, 3.0, etc.).	1
12. Multiply line 11 by line 6 by line 9.	129″
13. Divide line 12 by 36″ and round up to the nearest ⅛ yard to determine the fabric yardage. Add ½ yard (1 yard for large windows) if you are sewing tabs from the same fabric. Allow extra yardage if the fabric has a repeat that you want to match.	4⅛ yards
14. For lining only: Repeat steps 10–13 to calculate the lining yardage.	n/a

Worksheet

PANEL SIZE	MY MEASUREMENTS AND CALCULATIONS (USE A CALCULATOR)
1. Enter your length measurement.	
2. Enter your width measurement.	
3. Measure the circumference of your curtain rod and add 1″.	
4. Circle the desired fullness. For tab curtains, allow 1½ or 2 times the width. This allows for some draping at the window when the curtains are drawn. For rod pocket curtains, allow 2 or 2½ times the width, or even more if the fabric is sheer.	1½ 2 2½
5. Multiply line 2 by line 4.	
6. Do you want one or two panels? (circle one) One Panel Two Panels	1 OR 2
7. Divide line 5 by line 6. The result is the finished panel width.	
8. Add two side hem allowances to line 7 (refer to the Hem Allowance chart on page 47). This is the panel width before hemming.	
9. Add the top and bottom hem allowances to line 1 (refer to the Hem Allowance chart) and the rod measurement for rod pocket panels (your answer to line 3 above). This is the panel length before hemming.	
FABRIC YARDAGE	
10. The width of your fabric is	
11. Using a calculator, divide line 8 by line 10. If the answer is 1 or less than 1, enter 1. If the answer is more than 1, round up to the nearest 0.5 decimal (1.5, 2.0, 2.5, 3.0, etc.).	
12. Multiply line 11 by line 6 by line 9.	
13. Divide line 12 by 36″ and round up to the nearest ⅛ yard to determine the fabric yardage. Add ½ yard (1 yard for large windows) if you are sewing tabs from the same fabric. Allow extra yardage if the fabric has a repeat that you want to match.	
14. For lining only: Repeat steps 10–13 to calculate the lining yardage.	

Hem Allowance

	LINED			UNLINED		
	TABS OR RINGS	ROD POCKET	ROD POCKET with 1″ self ruffle	TABS OR RINGS	ROD POCKET	ROD POCKET with 1″ self ruffle
SIDES (each)	½″	½″	½″	1¼″	1¼″	1¼″
TOP	1″	Rod Measurement + ½″	Rod Measurement + 2½″	½″	Rod Measurement + ½″	Rod Measurement + 2½″
BOTTOM	4″	4″	4″	4″	4″	4″

Fabric Selection

Think about the room and how you want the curtains to function. Do you need privacy but still crave light? Light-filtering sheers may be the answer for you. Do you want to conceal or enhance the view to the outdoors? Do you want the curtains to be a focal point, or should they quietly blend into the room? You will want to consider these points as you select the style and fabric for the curtain.

Fabrics for curtains can be plain or multicolored, opaque or sheer. You can use just about any fiber type, including cottons, blends, synthetics, and natural fibers like linen or wool. Solid-colored fabrics will blend in with the room and be restful to look at. A patterned fabric can help draw the eye away from unappealing design features in the room. For high drama, choose curtains that make a sharp contrast against the wall color. Be careful, though. Remember that curtains for a large window require a lot of fabric. Too much color or pattern can be overpowering. Look through home furnishing books and magazines for window treatment ideas to help you make appropriate choices.

Lining or Not?

Curtains can be lined or not—the choice is up to you. An unlined curtain is informal and casual and suits today's lifestyle. But there are times when a lining may be desirable. A heavy lining can block out the light, ensuring total privacy during day or night. Linings can shield against sun exposure that would fade or weaken the curtain fabric. If the curtains in several rooms are sewn from different fabrics, lining them all will give the windows a uniform appearance when the house is viewed from the outside. If you choose a lightweight or delicate fabric for the curtain, a lining can give it extra body and drape.

Many fabric stores carry a variety of fabrics especially designed for lining curtains. Both lined and unlined curtains are easy to sew.

How Much Fabric?

After you have determined the panel size and selected a fabric, a final step is to calculate the fabric yardage. In a curtain panel, the selvages run vertically. Sometimes you will be able to cut the curtain panel from one width of fabric. Other times you may have to sew two or more pieces of fabric together to obtain the panel width you need. Complete Worksheet lines 10–13 (page 46) to calculate the yardage for your panels. In line 10, enter the width of the fabric you have chosen. Quilting cottons are typically 42″ wide, whereas decorator fabrics are 54″ to 60″ wide.

Sewing the Panels
Unlined Panels

1. If your answer to Worksheet line 11 is 1, skip ahead to step 3. If your answer to Worksheet line 11 is 1.5, 2.5, or 3.5, cut one of the fabric pieces in half along the lengthwise grain.

2. Lay out the fabric pieces for each panel side by side. Sew the pieces, right sides together, along the lengthwise grain, starting at the top and using a ½″ seam allowance. Press the seam allowances open.

3. Trim the width of each curtain panel to match your measurement from Worksheet line 8. Fold and press the side edges of each panel ¼″ to the wrong side. Fold again 1″ and press. On some fabrics, you may prefer to lightly mark the fold lines on the wrong side before pressing; use a pencil for light fabrics and a white chalk pencil for dark fabrics. Topstitch along the first fold with matching thread.

4. Fold and press the bottom edge of each panel 2″ to the wrong side. Fold again 2″ and press. Topstitch.

Hem Measuring

To mark a long edge for hemming, measure from the raw edge every 12″ to 14″ and mark the fabric lightly with a pencil or chalk. Then place a long ruler or yardstick on the marks and draw a connecting line.

Lined Panels

Lined panels can be made with tabs, rings, or a rod pocket along the header. Follow the steps below to make a simple lined panel. Instructions for various header treatments are in the project recipes.

1. Follow steps 1–2 of Unlined Panels (page 47) for each curtain panel. Repeat for each lining panel.

2. Trim the width of each curtain panel to match your measurement from Worksheet line 8. Trim the width and length of each lining panel to 1″ less than the curtain panel.

3. Complete step 4 of Unlined Panels (above) to hem each curtain panel and each lining panel.

4. Place a curtain panel and lining panel right sides together, matching the top edges and the edges along one side. Note that the lining hem is 1″ shorter than the curtain hem. Stitch the side seam,

Stabilizing Tip

Fuse lightweight interfacing to the wrong side of the header to help stabilize lightweight fabrics.

using a ½″ seam allowance. Press toward the lining. Align the raw edges on the opposite side and stitch together. Press toward the lining.

5. Realign the top raw edges, right sides together, so that the lining is centered. The side seams will roll in toward the lining by ¼″. Stitch the top seam. Turn the lined curtain panel right side out. Press. Topstitch if desired.

6. If creating a rod pocket, leave the lining and curtain panel side seams open for 2″ to 3″ where the rod will be located. After you have turned and pressed the panels, topstitch the edges, backstitching to leave openings for the rod. Topstitch across the panels once (or twice, for a ruffled header) to create the channel for the rod.

Sewing the Header

Note: The instructions that follow are for unlined curtain panels.

Tabs

Use the leftover curtain fabric to make the facing and tabs.

1. Cut two 2½″-wide strips of the leftover fabric on the crosswise grain. Sew the strips together end to end. Press the seams open. Cut and join more strips until the total length of the strip exceeds the total width of the panels.

2. Subcut the strip into one facing strip per panel, making each facing 1″ longer than the panel width. Press the ends and one long edge of each facing ½″ to the wrong side.

3. Divide the width of each panel by 6″, 7″, or 8″ (the approximate spacing between tabs) and round up (if necessary) to the nearest whole number. The result is the number of tabs you should make. Example: A panel that is 30″ wide would require 4 or 5 tabs. Choose the number of tabs you would like to use. Insert pins along the top raw edge of each panel to mark the placement of the tabs.

4. Cut one 5″-wide strip of the leftover fabric on the crosswise grain. Subcut into 7″-long tab strips. Repeat until you have one tab strip for each tab. Fold each tab strip in half lengthwise, right sides and long raw edges together. Stitch a ½″ seam. Turn right side out and press, centering the seam on one side.

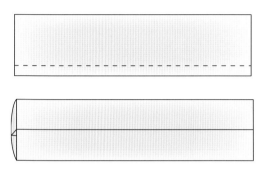

Tip

A 7″-long tab will fit around most curtain drapery rods with enough leeway for easy gliding. If the diameter of your rod is extra large, you may need or prefer a longer tab. Drape a tape measure over the rod. Measure from 1″ below the rod on one side to 1″ below the rod on the other side. Add 1″ for seam allowances to the total to determine the length of the tab strip.

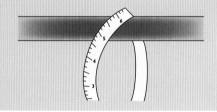

5. Fold each tab in half, raw edges together. On the right side of the curtain panel, pin a tab to the raw edge of the panel at each pin marker. Measure to make sure the tabs are evenly spaced.

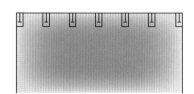

6. Place the unfolded edge of the facing on the curtain panel, right sides together. Stitch ½″ from the edge, trapping the tabs in the seam allowance. Turn the facing to the wrong side and press. Topstitch the prepressed ½″ hems on the side and bottom edges of the facing.

Rings

Use the leftover curtain fabric to make the facing and ring tabs.

1. Follow step 1 of Tabs (page 48) to cut and join the facing strips.

2. Follow step 2 of Tabs to subcut and press the facing strips.

3. Follow step 3 of Tabs to mark the location of the ring tabs with pins.

4. Follow step 4 of Tabs, but make the tabs only 4″ long, do not fold them in half, and pin only one end to the panel at each pin marker.

5. Follow step 6 of Tabs to join the facing to the panel; press and topstitch.

6. Fold the tabs through the rings and to the back of the facing. Fold under the raw end and hand tack in place. (Alternatively, if the rings are washable, you can fold them inside the tabs and sew both ends of the tabs into the header permanently.)

Rod Pocket

1. Lay the unlined curtain panel wrong side up. Press the raw top edge ¼″ to the wrong side.

2. Refer to the Hem Allowance chart (page 47). Measure from the top edge and mark a line for the finished top edge. Fold down on the marked line and press.

3. Topstitch along the lower folded edge, as shown, to form the rod pocket.

4. For a self ruffle, topstitch a second row of stitching 1″ from the top folded edge.

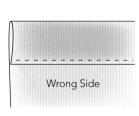
Rod Pocket

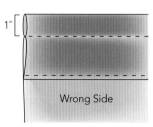
Rod Pocket With Self Ruffle

curtain
recipes

café curtain with tabs

This sheer single-panel café curtain provides a comfortable balance of privacy and natural light in a powder room. Decorative buttons accent the tabs, which are sewn with a point at one end. The tabs hang from an inside mount rod, and the bottom hem just touches the windowsill.

Sew all seams using a $\frac{1}{2}''$ seam allowance.

MEASURING: Follow steps 1–5 of Measuring (page 44).

SIZING THE PANELS: Complete the Worksheet (page 46) and cut the fabric. Note that the curtain shown is a single panel that spans the width of the window.

SEWING THE PANELS: Follow steps 1–4 of Unlined Panels (page 47).

TABS: Follow steps 1–6 of Tabs (page 48), except for these modifications:

When making the tabs, after you sew the vertical seam, shift the seam to the center (while wrong side out) and sew a point on one end. Taking one stitch across the end rather than turning sharply will make it easier to turn. Trim the excess fabric around the point and turn the tab to the right side; press.

Sew the straight end of the tab into the top of the panel, seam side down. When the facing is turned and topstitched, bring the pointed end to the front of the panel and hand tack it in place. Buttons may be added for a decorative accent.

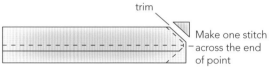

trim

Make one stitch across the end of point

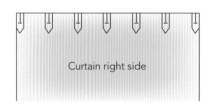

Curtain right side

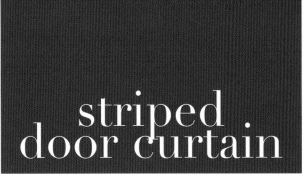

striped door curtain

This lined tab curtain is used in place of a door to cover the entry to a closet. It is pieced from bands of fabric in four different colors to create a striped effect. Each color band has its own matching tab along the header. The curtain for the double door opening can be sewn as one or two panels.

Materials

CURTAIN SIZE	FABRIC 1	FABRIC 2	FABRIC 3	FABRIC 4	LINING
Single Door Opening (30″ × 81″)	2½ yards each				4¾ yards
Double Door Opening (60″ × 81″)	2½ yards each				7¼ yards

Cutting Guide

CURTAIN SIZE	COLOR BANDS	TABS	LINING
Single Door Curtain Panel (48″ × 81″)	7″ × 85½″ (cut 2 of each fabric)	2½″ × 15″ (cut 1 strip of each fabric)	42″ × 84½″ (cut 2)
Double Door Curtain Panel (96″ × 81″)	7″ × 85½″ (cut 4 of each fabric)	2½″ × 30″ (cut 1 strip of each fabric)	42″ × 84½″ (cut 3)

Sew all seams using a ½″ seam allowance.

MEASURING: Measure the length and width of your closet opening. Adjust the panel lengths in the Cutting Guide, if necessary. You can ignore slight discrepancies in the panel width. Mount the curtain rod 2″ above the door opening.

CUTTING: Cut the color bands, tab strips, and lining pieces on the lengthwise grain, as directed in the Cutting Guide.

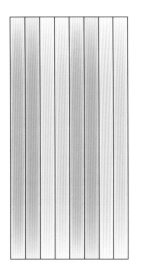

SEWING THE PANELS: Lay out the color bands side by side in a repeat pattern, as shown in the photograph. Sew each color band to its neighbor, right sides together. Press. For the double door size, you can join all 16 color bands into one panel or you can make two panels of 8 color bands each.

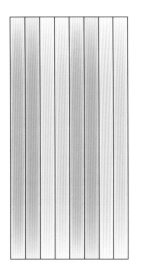

Single Door Panel   Double Door Panel   Double Door, Two Panels

SEWING THE LINING: Sew the lining pieces right sides together along the lengthwise grain. Press. Trim the lining to the following dimensions:

Single Door: 48″ × 84$\frac{1}{2}$″

Double Door, One Panel: 96″ × 84$\frac{1}{2}$″

Double Door, Two Panels: 48″ × 84$\frac{1}{2}$″ each

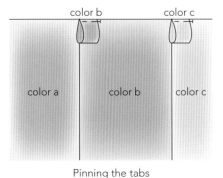

Pinning the tabs

TABS: Subcut each tab strip into 5″-long pieces. Follow step 4 of Tabs (page 49) to sew the tabs. Fold each tab in half and pin the raw edges to the header so they are even with the color band seams. At the left edge, pin a tab $\frac{1}{2}$″ in from the edge. At the right edge, pin an extra tab, in a matching color, also $\frac{1}{2}$″ from the edge. Complete steps 3–5 of Lined Panels (page 48), trapping the tabs in the header seam.

ruffled valance

A valance is a decorative accent—a mini curtain—placed at the top of the window. Valances look pretty when paired with cafe curtains. They can also camouflage shades or blinds when they are in the rolled-up position. The valance shown here is hung from a spring-loaded rod mounted inside the window frame.

Sew all seams using a ½″ seam allowance.

MEASURING: Follow steps 1–5 of Measuring (page 44).

SIZING THE PANELS: Complete the Worksheet (page 46) and cut the fabric. Note that a valance is a single panel that spans the width of the window.

SEWING THE PANELS: Follow steps 1–4 of Unlined Panels (page 47).

SEWING THE HEADER: Follow steps 1–4 of Rod Pocket (page 49).

curtain with rings

Rings are a variation on the tab header. Metal rings move easily along the rod and make a pleasing jingling sound. Many people prefer rings to tabs for curtains that will be opened and closed frequently. In the curtain shown here, the rings are joined to the header with tiny tabs.

Sew all seams using a ½″ seam allowance.

MEASURING: Follow steps 1–5 of Measuring (page 44).

SIZING THE PANELS: Complete the Worksheet (page 46) for an unlined panel with tabs. Cut the fabric for the panels.

SEWING THE PANELS: Follow steps 1–4 of Unlined Panels (page 47).

TABS: Complete steps 1–6 of Rings (page 49).

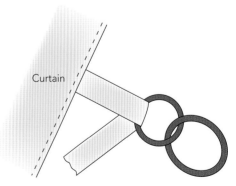

Curtain

curtain with tiebacks

Think of tiebacks as a helping hand. They draw the curtain back and hold it in place to reveal the view. This tieback is sewn from solid brown fabric and trimmed with pink braid and rickrack. The warm colors and tropical print create the perfect indoor ambiance for viewing the white pine foliage outside.

Tieback Materials

	FABRIC TRIM	FLAT BRAID TRIM	RICKRACK	CUP HOOKS AND PLASTIC CROCHET RINGS
FOR TWO 24″ × 3″ TIEBACKS:	½ yard	1½ yards	3 yards	2 of each

Sew all seams using a ½″ seam allowance.

MEASURING: Follow steps 1–5 of Measuring (page 44).

SIZING THE PANELS: Complete the Worksheet (page 46) for an unlined curtain with a rod pocket. Cut the fabric for the panels.

SEWING THE PANELS: Follow steps 1–3 of Unlined Panels (page 47).

ROD POCKET: Complete steps 1–3 of Rod Pocket (page 49).

TIEBACKS: Cut 2 strips 7″ × 24″ of fabric.

1. Fold each strip in half, aligning the long raw edges, right sides together. Sew each strip along the long edges. Turn them right side out.

2. Put the seam to one edge and topstitch a length of rickrack along that edge. Sew a matching strip of rickrack along the opposite edge.

3. Measure and topstitch a length of braid along the center of the strip.

4. For each tieback, turn the short ends (with trim) to the back ½″ and topstitch. Fold the tieback in half loosely, forming a loop. Tack the ends together, trim side out, and hand sew a plastic crochet ring to the joined ends.

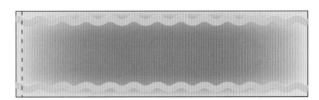

5. Mount a small cup hook in the window sill (specialty hooks are also available at some fabric or curtain stores). Slip the curtain inside the tieback and slip the plastic ring over the hook. Arrange the curtain and tieback in front of the hook so it is not noticeable.

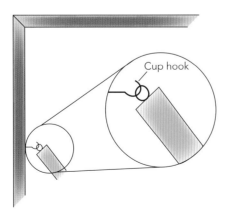

Cup hook

patchwork shower curtain

Four different fabrics create a pleasing diagonal color flow on this patchwork shower curtain. The outer border, sewn from a fifth fabric, frames the design. Buttonholes sewn across the header allow the curtain to hang from standard or decorative shower rod rings.

Patchwork Diagram

PATCHWORK: Lay out the blocks in 6 rows of 6 blocks each to form a diagonal pattern. Stitch the blocks together in rows, using a $1/2''$ seam allowance. Press the seams open. Join the rows. Press.

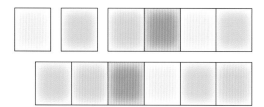

Patchwork Assembly

BORDERS: Sew the side borders to the patchwork. Press toward the borders. Fuse the interfacing strips to the wrong side of the top border, overlapping the ends a scant $1/8''$. Sew the top and bottom borders to the patchwork. Press. Fold and press a $2''$ hem on the bottom border. Topstitch.

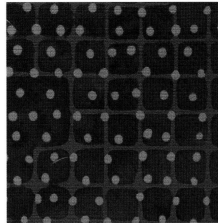
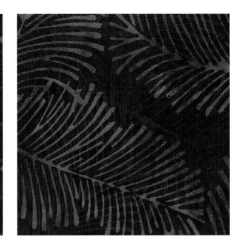

Materials

FABRIC 1	1⅜ yards
FABRIC 2	1 yard
FABRIC 3	1 yard
FABRIC 4	1 yard
FABRIC 5 FOR BORDER	1½ yards
LINING FABRIC	4¼ yards
LIGHTWEIGHT FUSIBLE INTERFACING	½ yard
SHOWER CURTAIN LINER	70″ × 72″

LINING: Join the lining panels together along a long edge. Press. Fold and press a 2″ hem on the bottom edge of the lining. Topstitch.

ASSEMBLY: Layer the patchwork and lining right sides together, matching the raw edges. Note that the lining hem is 1″ shorter than the patchwork hem. Stitch the side and top edges, using a ½″ seam allowance. Trim the corners diagonally. Turn right side out and press.

BUTTONHOLES: Lay the shower curtain right side up. Layer a shower curtain liner on top, offsetting the top and side edges by ¼″. Use the liner header as a template. Use a pencil (for light fabrics) or a white chalk pencil (for dark fabrics) to mark the curtain ring hole placement on the top border of the patchwork curtain. Sew a buttonhole at each mark, referring to your sewing machine instruction manual.

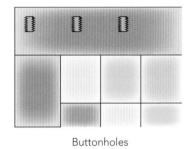

Buttonholes

HANGING THE CURTAIN: Hang the liner and shower curtain from one set of shower rod hooks or rings. Make sure the liner faces the shower stall or tub.

Cutting Guide

	FABRIC 1	FABRIC 2	FABRIC 3	FABRIC 4	FABRIC 5	LINING	INTERFACING
Strips/Panels	11¼″ × 42″ (cut 4)	11¼″ × 42″ (cut 3)	11¼″ × 42″ (cut 3)	11¼″ × 42″ (cut 3)	5¾″ × 42″; (cut 7) piece end to end to make one long strip	38″ × 73″ (cut 2)	5¾″ × 36″ strips (cut 2)
Subcuts	11¼″ × 11¾″ blocks (cut 10)	11¼″ × 11¾″ blocks (cut 9)	11¼″ × 11¾″ blocks (cut 8)	11¼″ × 11¾″ blocks (cut 9)	5¾″ × 65½″ side borders (cut 2) 5¾″ × 72″ top and bottom borders (cut 2)		

classic
shower curtain

Just a few yards of fabric can transform a clear shower curtain liner into beautiful home decor. Sew right through the plastic to make this ingenious bathroom accent.

Sew all seams using a $\frac{1}{2}''$ seam allowance.

MEASURING: Measure the shower stall or bathtub opening. Purchase a rod and shower curtain liner to fit the opening. Install the rod at the desired height, following the manufacturer's instructions.

SIZING THE PANEL: Measure the length and width of the liner. Add $2\frac{1}{2}''$ to the width and 10″ to the length for the hem allowances. Enter the width and length into Worksheet lines 8 and 9 (page 46). Complete Worksheet lines 10–13 to calculate the fabric yardage.

SEWING THE PANEL: Complete steps 1–3 of Unlined Panels (page 47).

ATTACHING THE LINER: Press the top raw edge of the fabric panel $\frac{1}{4}''$ to the wrong side. Fold down the top edge 3″ to the wrong side and press. Place the header of the liner on this folded hem, 1″ below the edge. Stitch through all the layers from the liner side at the bottom of the liner header. Use polyester thread, a fine machine needle, and a longer-than-usual stitch length.

HANGING THE CURTAIN: Hang the curtain by the liner, using shower rod hooks or rings. Fold the loose flap of fabric forward to form a self valance. For a sturdier header, fold the fabric flap over the liner. Install grommets along the edge using a grommet tool (available at fabric or hardware stores). Space the grommets to match the hole spacing on the liner. Or make buttonholes in the fabric to line up with the holes in the liner.

index

sources

FABRIC AND SUPPLIES

The Stitchin' Post
PO Box 280
311 West Cascade
Sisters, OR 97759
541 549 6061
www.stitchinpost.com
stitchin@stitchinpost.com

The Cotton Patch
1025 Brown Avenue, Dept CTB
Lafayette, CA 94549
www.quiltusa.com
cottonpatch@quiltusa.com

HOME ACCESSORIES

The Wild Hare
PO Box 280
321 West Cascade
Sisters, OR 97759
541 549 6061

Oh Sew Easy Duvet Covers & Curtains

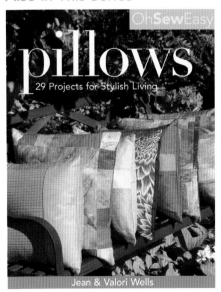

ABOUT THE AUTHORS

Jean Wells and her daughter Valori Wells are a well-known duo involved in quiltmaking, fabric design, and operating The Stitchin' Post in Sisters, Oregon.

Jean established this "destination" quilt shop in 1975 and has since won many awards for her business and quilting skills. She has traveled extensively, giving lectures, teaching workshops, and sharing her love of sewing with thousands of quilters worldwide. She is the founder of the annual Sisters Outdoor Quilt Show.

When Valori was in college, she and Jean began collaborating on quilting books with a garden flair. Valori's talents as a photographer captured nature at its best, and her inspirational images soon became the focus of her own distinctive quilting style. Her career came into full blossom when she began designing fabrics for the quilting industry. Valori returned to Sisters seven years ago to join her mother in managing the store. Currently she is a designer for Free Spirit Textiles.

Both women have been spreading their wings in the direction of soft furnishings. *Oh Sew Easy Duvet Covers & Curtains* is the second book in their new series devoted to sewing projects for the home. Valori and her husband Ross recently welcomed their first child, Olivia Rose, into their family. Jean and husband John live just outside Sisters, Oregon, where they have a large garden.

Also in This Series

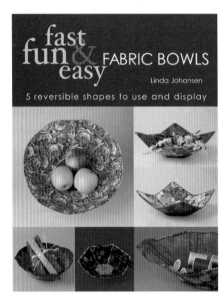
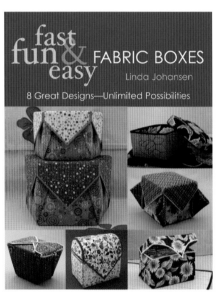
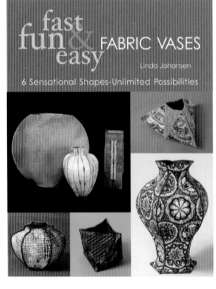

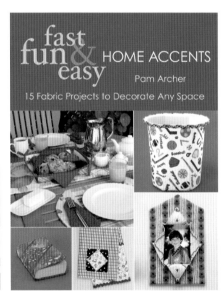